MARIAH CAREY

A Real-Life Reader Biography

Melanie Cole

Mitchell Lane Publishers, Inc.
P.O. Box 200 • Childs, Maryland 21916

Mitchell Lane
PUBLISHERS

First Printing

Real-Life Reader Biographies

Selena	Robert Rodriguez	**Mariah Carey**	Rafael Palmeiro
Tommy Nuñez	Trent Dimas	Cristina Saralegui	Andres Galarraga
Oscar De La Hoya	Gloria Estefan	Jimmy Smits	Mary Joe Fernandez
Cesar Chavez	Isabel Allende	Carlos Mencia	Jaime Escalante

Library of Congress Cataloging-in-Publication Data
Cole, Melanie, 1957–
   Mariah Carey / Melanie Cole.
     p. cm. — (A real-life reader biography)
   Chronology: p.
   Includes index.
   Summary: Presents a biography of one of the best-selling recording artists of the 1990s, whose vocal styles are drawn from gospel and rhythm and blues.
   ISBN 1-883845-51-3 (library)
   1. Carey, Mariah—Juvenile literature. 2. Singers—United States—Biography—Juvenile literature.
[1. Carey, Mariah. 2. Singers. 3. Women—Biography.] I. Title. II. Series.
ML3930.C257C65 1997
782.42164′092—dc21
[B]
                                                                          97-21843
                                                                                     CIP
                                                                                   AC MN

ABOUT THE AUTHOR: Melanie Cole has been a writer and editor for seventeen years. She has been an associate editor of *Texas Monthly* and is now managing editor of *Hispanic* magazine. She has published poems, articles, and reviews in various journals, magazines, and newspapers. She is also a contributing writer to **Famous People of Hispanic Heritage** (Mitchell Lane). Originally from Kansas, Ms. Cole now lives in Austin, Texas.

PHOTO CREDITS: cover: AP Photo/The Los Angeles Times, Robert Gauthier; p. 4 sketch by Barbara Tidman; pp. 23, 25 AP Photos; pp. 14, 18, 20 Reuters/Corbis-Bettmann; p. 27 Archive Photos; p. 29 Rose Hartman, Globe Photos; p. 30 James M. Kelley, Globe Photos

ACKNOWLEDGMENTS: The following story has been thoroughly researched and checked for accuracy. To the best of our knowledge, it represents a true story. Though we attempted to contact each person profiled in our Real-Life Reader Biographies, for various reasons, we were unable to authorize every story.

Table of Contents

Chapter 1
Young Mariah

Singer Mariah Carey was born March 27, 1970, on Long Island, New York. Music was a part of her life from the beginning. She was even named after a song: "They Call the Wind Mariah" from the musical *Paint Your Wagon*.

Mariah was the third of three children born to Patricia Hickey Carey and Alfred Roy Carey. Patricia and Alfred had had a son, Morgan, in 1961 and a daughter, Alison, in 1962. Morgan and Alison

Music was always a part of Mariah Carey's life.

were ten and nine when Mariah was born.

Mariah's heritage is a mix of races. Her mother is Irish and her father is African-American and Venezuelan. Mariah identifies with the groups that make up her heritage. But she doesn't favor one group over another. "I am a human being, a person," she states.

There was much racism in the sixties, and people treated Alfred and Patricia unfairly because they were a mixed-race couple. The strain on them was too much. Mariah's parents divorced in 1972, when Mariah was two years old. Mariah's sister, Alison, chose to live with her father. Her brother, Morgan, lived for a while with each parent.

Mariah, Morgan, and Alison also endured a great deal of

prejudice when they were growing up. Their dogs were poisoned and their cars were set on fire. The neighborhood kids would shout racial slurs. Sometimes they would beat up the Carey children. For a while, Mariah lived with her African-American grandmother, but she felt different there, too. Because Mariah's skin is lighter than that of many other African-Americans, the neighborhood children would call her white girl.

Mariah was raised mostly by her mother. A working mom, Patricia supported the family by giving voice lessons. She also had a job singing for the New York Metropolitan Opera. She was a classically trained mezzo soprano (which means she sang in the middle range of the highest woman's part).

Mariah knew she wanted to be a singer from the time she was a small girl.

Mariah knew she wanted to be a singer from the time she was a small girl. It was the only dream she had. When she was young, she loved writing poems. Whether she was feeling happy or sad, she liked to express her feelings in her poems. Since she also loved to sing, it wasn't long before she combined the poems with tunes she made up in her head. This was how she started writing songs—first the words, or lyrics, and then the tune.

By the time she was in junior high, Mariah was actively writing songs and lyrics, but she did so secretly. No one knew that the shy girl was writing songs in her notebook every night after school. As she got older, many of her songs were about love and relationships.

Chapter 2
Songbird

As a little girl, Mariah could imitate almost any sound she heard. When she heard a song on the radio, she could sing it. She often heard her mother giving voice lessons. Her mother also sang all the time.

Mariah's amazing talent was clear from an early age. Mariah's mother said, "From the time Mariah was a tiny girl, she sang on true pitch; she was able to hear a sound and duplicate it exactly."

"From the time Mariah was a tiny girl, she sang on true pitch."

One day, while her mother was practicing a very hard song, she forgot where she was supposed to start singing. Exactly where her mother was supposed to sing little Mariah piped up—in Italian. She was only three years old. She didn't understand Italian, but she had learned her mother's part perfectly.

Her mother gave her singing lessons.

In 1974, Patricia began giving Mariah singing lessons. But she let Mariah sing whatever kinds of songs she wanted to. She never forced her to sing opera. Mariah loved listening to popular music on the radio. She liked Motown hits, rhythm and blues (R&B), and jazz. Sometimes she played her mother's old records from the sixties. This older music influenced the kinds of songs Mariah recorded later.

While she was still in high school, Mariah was writing and

recording songs with a friend. For her sixteenth birthday, her brother, Morgan, gave her the money to make a demo tape. This tape was to show how good her voice sounded and what kinds of songs she was able to sing. Demo tapes are given to record producers in the hope that a producer will want the performer to make an album.

Remembering high school, Mariah says she preferred her quiet writing time. "When I was at home, I was listening to music and writing songs." She observed that most of her friends liked to talk about what they would do when they grew up, including getting married and having babies. Instead, Mariah talked about music.

Mariah was always focused on music. In fact, she spent her time and energy practicing her music

For her sixteenth birthday, her brother, Morgan, gave her the money to make a demo tape.

> **Mariah moved to New York City to follow her dream of becoming a recording artist.**

instead of on her schoolwork. Her teachers tried to get her to focus on her studies, but Mariah only wanted to concentrate on her music. When she graduated from Harborfields High School on Long Island in 1987, she went off to start her singing career.

Mariah moved to New York City to follow her dream. She shared a tiny apartment with two other girls who also dreamed of becoming performers. She worked as a waitress, a hatcheck girl, a restaurant hostess, and a hair salon assistant in order to have money for food. When she wasn't working, she walked around to every record company in town, trying to get them to listen to her demo tape.

Chapter 3
Big Break

One day in November 1988, Mariah went to a party with one of her girlfriends. While she was there, she met a man who worked at a recording company. The man's name was Tommy Mottola. He was president of Sony Music Entertainment, parent company of Columbia Records. Mariah told him her dream was to become a pop singer. She gave him her demo tape.

After leaving the party, Tommy listened to Mariah's tape in his car.

Mariah gave Tommy Mottola, president of Sony Music, her demo tape.

What he heard was a clear voice with incredible range. He was so excited about Mariah's voice that he asked his driver to turn the limousine around. He went back to the party to try to find her. She had already left.

Tommy Mottola had a good ear for talent. He told a newspaper writer in 1991, "When I heard and saw Mariah, there was absolutely no doubt she was in every way destined for stardom."

It wasn't hard to find Mariah the next day. Mariah signed a contract with Sony to make records. She set to work recording her first album, *Mariah Carey*, which showed off her smooth, five-octave voice. She also starred in music videos.

Sony released *Mariah Carey* in 1990. The album shot to number one on the *Billboard* chart. It also

Mariah signed a contract with Sony to make records.

won two Grammy Awards that year—for best female pop vocal performance and best new artist.

On her next albums, Mariah was able to do more than just sing songs the way the record company wanted them. She did more composing. She also began producing her own songs. That meant she could control how all the other voices and instruments would work together on the final recording. Unlike other pop stars, such as Whitney Houston and Madonna, Mariah writes and produces most of her own songs.

Her second album, *Emotions*, released in 1991, made it to number four on the *Billboard* album chart. Next was *MTV Unplugged EP*, released in 1992. It peaked at number three on the *Billboard* album chart.

Mariah composes and produces her own songs.

Mariah Carey holds her two Grammys at the 33rd annual Grammy Awards in New York, February 20, 1991.

Chapter 4
Cinderella Story

In the fairy tale of Cinderella, a poor unknown girl who is truly talented and beautiful meets a prince. She marries this prince and they live happily ever after. Mariah Carey's story is a lot like Cinderella's, except that Mariah's "prince" was a record producer—the very rich and powerful Tommy Mottola, the man she had met at the party and who had "discovered" her talent.

Tommy and Mariah started out as business partners, but then they

Mariah's prince was Tommy Mottola.

Mariah arrived for her wedding at St. Thomas Episcopal Church in Manhattan, June 5, 1993. Barbra Streisand, Billy Joel, and Bruce Springsteen were among the guests.

fell in love with each other. At first, they tried to keep it quiet. Tommy was a big record executive. He had discovered Mariah. There was also a big difference in their ages. They did not want anyone to know they were dating. But once the wedding date was set, they could not keep the secret any longer. Mariah was very happy about her upcoming marriage. "It really is like Cinderella," she said.

On Saturday, June 5, 1993, Mariah married Tommy. It was a storybook wedding. They married in an Episcopalian church in New York City. She wore a gown similar to the one England's Princess Diana had worn. The train on Mariah's gown was so long it took six "ladies–in–waiting" to bring it into the church. Mariah had come a long way from the days when she was running around New York dropping off demo tapes.

Getting married did not slow her down.

Getting married did not slow her down. Mariah continued to release one album a year: her fourth album, *Music Box*, in August 1993; her fifth, *Merry Christmas*, in November 1994; and her sixth, *Daydream*, in 1995.

Chapter 5
Star and Producer

Mariah has had her share of lucky breaks. However, she has succeeded because of her talent and hard work. She is the biggest-selling female singer of the 1990s. Since her first album was released, she has sold more than 80 million albums worldwide (as of April 1996). Three of her albums went to number one. She has released eleven number-one singles on the pop music chart and five number-one rhythm and blues singles.

Mariah has succeeded because of her talent and hard work.

Mariah loves animals. She has horses, four dogs, and two Persian cats. Until her separation from her husband in 1997, Mariah lived with Tommy in a big home. Their home was like a palace. Actually, they had two homes: an apartment in Manhattan and a big house in upstate New York, in the Hudson River Valley. It was about an hour and a half from New York City.

Mariah has many things now that she lacked when she was growing up. Yet, she likes to lead a "normal" life. "When I have a minute to reflect," she says, "I realize that my life has been pretty amazing. But I consider myself a normal person who wants a normal life. It's exciting to do what I do, but I also like to stay real and grounded."

Mariah has a devoted group of
fans. She has fan clubs in several
countries, including Australia. She

*Mariah Carey
sang on stage
during the 23rd
annual American
Music Awards,
January 29, 1996.*

has branched out to Europe and Asia as well. Her first five singles all reached number one on the *Billboard* Hot 100 chart. That was a feat never done before by any other artist—not even Elvis Presley or the Beatles. Mariah has made many award-winning music videos. And she directed many of them.

Mariah didn't release an album in 1996, but she appeared as a guest artist on several other artists' albums. One of these was the popular group Boyz II Men.

In February 1997, Sony Entertainment made an announcement. The company had created a new record label called Crave and Mariah would be in charge. Mariah said, "Our main goal is to have a close-knit label where artists can feel comfortable, where we can discover some great music and get it the attention it deserves." Mariah's label supports new artists. "Letting artists be themselves and getting their music

Mariah displays her awards for the best pop-rock female artist and best female in the soul rhythm and blues categories at the 23rd annual American Music Awards. The awards were held at Shrine Auditorium in Los Angeles in 1996.

out to people—that's what Crave is all about," she says. Crave signed the female vocal group Allure as its first artists. Allure's first single is "Head Over Heels."

Mariah will record and produce albums for many more years. "I don't want to be a 'big star,'" Mariah said, "but I want to be respected as an artist. . . . This is my love. I want to sing for the rest of my life."

Mariah does a lot of charity work. In 1994 she got involved with the Fresh Air Fund. She committed $1 million to support a career awareness camp. Called Camp Mariah, the program helps New York City children explore different life options and take part in summer camps. Mariah is a popular spokesperson for the program. She has visited the camp several times

Mariah is in charge of a new record label for Sony.

and has even taken part in a foot race with some of the kids. She also gave a benefit concert for the Fresh Air Fund on December 8, 1994.

Mariah and husband Tommy attended a benefit for the Fresh Air Fund in New York City on June 6, 1996. They were honorary chairmen at the event, which honored producer Quincy Jones and New Jersey Governor Christine Todd Whitman.

In addition to her work with the Fresh Air Fund, Mariah helps the Police Athletic League in Manhattan. In 1994, she also attended a Chanel fashion show and luncheon to benefit the obstetrics department of New York Hospital. "I try to be a good person," says Mariah, "and make a difference where I can." Most of Mariah's charity work involves children.

Mariah knew she wanted to be a singer from the age of four. She says her mother gave her confidence. Mariah has always known she could succeed. "Because my mom did it for a living when I was young, I knew it could be more than a pipe dream. . . . My mom always told me, 'You are special. You have a talent.' She gave me the belief that I could do this."

But Mariah could never have imagined the kind of success she would have with her voice. Even

Mariah attended a Chanel lunch and fashion show to benefit New York Hospital.

though she has separated from her husband, her popularity as a singer will continue. The poor Cinderella from New York has become a princess of popular music known all over the world.

Mariah sang at the 15th annual National Peace Officers Memorial Day Service in Washington, DC., 1996.

Discography

Selected Top Singles

"Visions of Love" (1990)
"Love Takes Time" (1990)
"Someday" (1991)
"I Don't Wanna Cry" (1991)
"Emotions" (1991)
"Can't Let Go" (1991)
"Make It Happen" (1992)
"I'll Be There" (1992)
"Dreamlover" (1993)
"Hero" (1993)
"Without You/Never Forget You" (1994)
"Anytime You Need a Friend" (1994)
"Endless Love" (duet with Luther Vandross, 1994)
"Fantasy" (1995)
"One Sweet Day" (1995)
"Open Arms" (1995)
"Always Be My Baby" (1995)

Albums

Mariah Carey (1990)
Emotions (1991)
MTV Unplugged EP (1992)
Music Box (1993)
Merry Christmas (1994)
Daydream (1995)

Chronology

- Born March 27, 1970, on Long Island, New York; mother: Patricia Hickey Carey; father: Alfred Roy Carey
- 1974, her mother began giving her singing lessons
- At 16, made a professional demo tape
- 1987, graduated from Harborfields High School on Long Island
- 1989, signed a recording contract with Columbia Records
- 1990, released first album, *Mariah Carey*, which won two Grammy Awards
- 1991–92, released second and third albums: *Emotions*, which she also produced, and *MTV Unplugged EP*
- June 1993, married Tommy Mottola in New York
- 1993–95, released fourth, fifth, and sixth albums: *Music Box*, *Merry Christmas*, and *Daydream*
- 1997, started her own record label, Crave.
- May 1997, Tommy Mottola and Mariah announced they were separating but would remain business partners and friends

Index